Part 1

Love, Loss & Peace

Nina Mtanu

Published by Nina Mtanu, 2024.

LOVE, LOSS & PEACE

First edition. September 5, 2024.

Copyright © 2024 Nina Mtanu.

ISBN: 979-8227475947

Written by Nina Mtanu.

Table of Contents

My aunt

You didn't live fast

You didn't love fast

You lived

And I admire that about you.

THIS LOVE

NINA MTANU

What is love?

Some say it is turbulent
It is horrid
And it is wild
Some say it is the conner stone of it all
It is the flame that burned me
It takes all of you and mends
And it is gentle
Some say it is quiet like a mouse
It is loud like an eruption
It is a rebirth
It conquers
And it is old
Some say it stings for eons
It is gentle like the landing of a butterfly
It is a gift
It steals all of your senses
Some say it is a myth
It exists
It is beautiful
And it is a phenomenon

Wandering finds

You claim to be lost
Wandering these halls
Melodies hang on balconies calling
And
Primed I bask nightly for a peek
Feignin' for a taste
Hanging on your telling breaths
I imagine your riddles delight
And
Words fill my lips

NINA MTANU

Heart scholar

Your light footsteps
Shake the dusty floors
Along the halls of my chambers
Dwarfed by secrets laden scrolls
You wander the citadel
Curious scholar laden with balms
Your gentle words incense
Perfumes I purchase for rainy days

Black love

Those bottomless brown eyes watch me
Gentle fingers caress my skin tenderly
Your mellow words drip over me
Patient and unhurried
As his strokes fill and crest
He thrusts us into frenzy
Our shimmering brown skin tangled in silks
Worshipping our love
Synching harmonies of pleas, we hold on
Delirious in our fevered lust
We transcend the confines of painful black love
Stitching and prying open pandoras box
We hurtle towards a new love
Uninhibited we make home in this new place
Naked and re-born
Gasping for breaths
We arch and twine
Tussling with past fears and denial
Denouncing sub-par efforts
We weep in the embrace of untainted love
Our crushing keens the binding soul signatures
Our laboured breaths ordain our vows as shaking bodies succumb
Black love thrives in lands without pain

NINA MTANU

Star crossed

In every galaxy we've crossed
We burn to a supernova
And our chaos aftermath
Lights their skies
Lead me home
With your glimmers
I've been waiting too long

LOVE, LOSS & PEACE

...

You wish for me to regale you
With words of how
How I love the shape of you
The softness of your skin
The valleys where my woes set
Your delicate hands that strangle my torment
And dainty legs that lift the weight of wails
Those lips pouring kind lullabies
But it is your soul that captivates
Razing through marrows of trauma
Muck smeared on my flesh I burn
Weary I have been your patient
And as I basked in your garden
Dug my fears into the fertile soil to bloom
I have found havens of Eden's meadow
Devout to dress you in petals of adoration
I slip notes to gods that we not part
Red string taught that I never wander alone

Tied

I'll kiss your palms
Leave lip prints on your
fingertips
Close my eyes and feel
The warmth of your palm on my cheek as
treats
I'll reach for you
Your whispers of adoration in my ear my
labryinth

Fierce love

Let me love you gently
Fiercely,
Even when the moment is bleak
Let me pour you the warmth from my cup
Restlessly,
Even when all else is nigh
Let me love you now
Presently,
Eventually I will be gone

Awaited

I watch the gate with a longing
Every night, I sit at the stoop and wait
Every dawn I wake missing you
Suspended in this space of longing
Anticipating your return
Anticipating your touch
Anticipating your call
Do you roam the wilds out there missing me?
Do you wish to one day walk home to me?
Do you believe I will still be here like before?
Do your days stretch long, like mine?
Nights bereft of your touch
Anniverseries contact close through a screen
Our re-union is a journal
Anticipating your reverent words
Anticipating your hands around me
Anticipating your undivided attention
I count the days until we embrace
I count the seconds until you're mine again
I count the blessings of knowing you
To love and be loved you eternally

...

Plunge me into the dark
Hide me in flutters
Of wild love
And call my name with fervour

NINA MTANU

Stirrings

Write me
In the dead of night
When your mind stirs
And your heart whispers my name

Adore

I will adore you
With words
With flowers
My presence
And when the warmth
Leaves you
I will hold you close
And pour mine 'til we burn

NINA MTANU

Old love

They think you ordinary
But I, who has
Searched
Waited
Wanted
Wished for the day
Honed the ways to tell you
Of your endless beauty and abundance
In words
As many as the grains of sand
For a place that has been time and time again
I, have shimmered in the winds
You are my ruins
Buried in the dunes and pristine
And only I know the secret doors to enter
I have walked down your halls
Followed echoes of your melody and yet
I know not all of you still
We rise and abscond from this world
Intune and unhurried by their mundane
Songs of love on our tongues as we wait
Deaths obssesion with life childs' play
This age old love steeps as millenias pass

Autographs

I'm covered in autographs
Of your adoration
But it's the love letter
Of your love's confession
Whispered with earnest
That I read over an over

...

Let them enjoy the fizzy parts of you
But I wish you cross my path
Aged and still
Steeped in rumours and secrets
I wish to feel your arrival before I see you
Carrying whirlwinds of bespoke noncholance,
When you pour yourself in this glass of my life
Wake my dulled senses
Filing the void with sound
Your laughs and smiles trinkets,
I will read the braille of your silences
Transcribe our calm in scripts
Filling my heart chambers with scrolls
Inked in hennas of Pharaoh's lines
As I erect the peaks of devotion divine
I don't want to love you mildly
Drown my unfathomed quirks in nods
Elation and celebration our communion

Borrowed time

Hearts a gallop
Grip a little tigher
Breaths shallow
We wait
Borrowing seconds
Your roaming eyes miss nothing
Words spilling over my lips in a rush
Our feverish kiss stretched out in denial
As we chase the timekeeper
Borrowing seconds
As the rails tremble
Chests filling fast
Creasting tears shinning
My hands cup your face
Tasting your tears and whispered love
Borrowing seconds

NINA MTANU

Blind love

Chase them
The excess kisses
Waiting, dripping, remaining
Be insatiable with me every minute
Let your heart run wild in my arms
Your name on my lips like a litany
Let your eyes roam over me free
Ravenously savage we take
And drink in these beats
My blinding love is
Courageous

I think about you in my most forlon times
Perched on tenderhooks of life's thunder
And i wish, for
Your tender words to untie me
Draping me over the sunny sounds of your song
My ears have grown blocked with remiss
Locked in the valleys of suffering
Nearing an edge of spirit death
The wettest rain upon my dried soul
Soften my edges so i can hold you close
To love you like the last drop of water
The wilds of extinction perilous but I be lucky to clutch life to my
bossom

NINA MTANU

Guests

Bright
You knock on my gloom
Calm
You shock my chaos
Slight
You block my venomous words
Weary
I armour my demons
Staying
You annex onto my journey

Deep breath

Your truths
And my keepsake lips
The willows of your chest
And my unabashed curiosity
Are like a deep breath
Drawn out in reception as we
Search where each hides their pain
Crouching highs and curled tight
Rattling keys golden glint
Running days as we
Study the healing of our love
Binding litanies wrapped bows

Timeless Love

I don't want this limited love
Having me for as long as you'll have me
Drinking from the dregs of your remnants
I want it all
I want your wildess
The eagerness to be exposed
Rushed at times but presently patient
Soaked in the feelings of unfathomable
Love 'til the end
Furious of the timekeeper
This cup sloshed over but never empty
I crave this muchness over droplets

...

Wrap me in wollen words
Of love's demise, enraptured
I dance unbothered, relieved
I've wished it true, to live
Body and soul tenured, wilful
Your love's grip hold, begile me
Lover
To die in your arms, I slumber
A thousand lives on your bossom, gleeful
To know your love, my
Keeper
Featured in *Reigningwordsnyc* read up

NINA MTANU

Tales of love

My eternity
Come sit upon my lap
And I will regale you
With tale of what we are
Meander into the valleys of our love
Propelled by the gust of truth
Like communion we have sustained
Shedding as seasons came and passed
I will tell you of the laughter
The memory of your tears on my fingertips
I sigh your name like a siren
Humming the melody of your gentle heart
The steel caps of your protective words
My eternity
Come lie beside me
And we will be alright as we depart

Molten love

Love me slow
Like the kindling of a fire
Let the sparks fly frequently
And when it burns
Let it engulf you
Blazing through the darkness
Light all the corners where my truth hides
Love me with a molten conviction
Sizzling under your devotion
Until we singe our names on the earth
Heat signatures roiling through time
Love me 'til the last breath

NINA MTANU

Wilds

In the silent hours of night
Sated and breathless
Limbs tangled in exhaustion
I want to be lost in the wilds of your words
Whispered hummed responses
Incomplete sentences of your fantasies
As your heavy eyes blink to keep sleep away
I want to get lost in the quiet of your peace
Huddled in one spot as we build futures
Absent fingers tracking all over my skin
Luxuriating in the mellowed moods of moonlight
I want to be lost in the wilds of your embrace.

Heaven without death

I won't kiss you with pity
But the reverence of a devout scholar
Steeped into the deep darks of you
The warrior who has slumbered in your caves
Fae wings mend under my care
I won't love you as if broken
Licking wounds and puring salt
Hurt to cause you pain
Riddled in healings of a thousand sutras
Long baths soul relaxing to unfurl
I won't leave your door closed
Ajar your mouth will pant loves licks
Lay you on petals of all bouquets your missed
I'll pick my dried tales and weave laughs
My bed will hug your soul bereft reach
Hands twined and love endless
My love a solace heaven without death
Featured in *Reigningwordsnyc* read up

NINA MTANU

Love's dance

We've traversed such vast spaces
From longing gazes across the room
Ravenous in our yearning as we wished
Leaning on corridors and chasing silhouettes
Scribbled letters littering bedside bins unsend
Palming hand prints on mirrors and sighing
Trussed moods awaiting a reply after post
Strings shortned as our voices came
Anxious meet ups morphed into stays
Eager eyes mapping every breath's hitch
Slowed walks crunching to the beats
Tentative hand grazes tracing groves
Courageous hand holds squeezing
Breathless gasps and eager hoping
Swelling anticipation into kisses
Quiet cuddles to boisterous hugs
Fervent motion layered with love
Seeking fingers and sucking lips
Bowing archs and indulging pets
Rousing praises and quiet hums
Distant yearns to present ties

Star gazing

Starlights
Ruminating night sighs
Wayward
Rushing songs lullabies
Shorelines
Ebbing promises
Settling
Haboured dreams and futures

NINA MTANU

Even now

Even now
When your spirit is weary
Trumpled upon by callousness
When your soul has grown tired
Even now
I see glitter in your beauty
When the words have died on your lips
Stiffled by unending taking over
When your voice has receeded
Even now
When hope seems distant
Wavering and thin like mist
When you don't believe in yourself anymore
Even now
When you don't see it, you shimmer
Kindness scattered around
I will collect all the pieces and put you back.

LOVE, LOSS & PEACE

...

I'll pour you
Rich brews of whispered litanies
Large servings of ravenous kisses
And warm caresses
Your sumptous tempest
For I can't hide this love I have for you

NINA MTANU

Drunked love

In dizzying spins, we ride
The rollercoaster of love, marionettes
Helpless, in the clutches of euphoria
Fall with me, string taught
Forlon, sense watches on
By the wayside

LOVE, LOSS & PEACE

In my arms

Pour the words on me
Liberated I will sing for you
Loved in this secluded spot we lie
Refusing to let it end
Forgoing change
I want us
Heated
Loving
Free

NINA MTANU

Great love

I don't want to die without a great love
I don't want to never know a giddy love
I don't want to never know delirious love
I want to look at someone and shiver
I want to simmer in that warm feeling
I want to be so sure of a love that is potent
To love so hard with surety
To be so enamoured with love
To be so selfless yet never run out of love
I want to love fearlessly
I want to look to my side and believe it all
I want the love that never fails, when the tide is high or low.

Love

This love, that fills me up
Filling gaps
Stitching loops
Cradling me in safety

NINA MTANU

...

Your love
Is my guillotine
March me up
To the podium of devotion
Charged sinner for my fear and evasion
Now bared to your love
I hang my running shoes
Armour and shield rusted
Newborn of love I depart
To die
A valiant death
Is a good death

Lost in you

I'd lick the words off you
Drunk, on their intoxication
Floating, on a swarm
Of greatness, as your voice cajoles me closer
Regale me with your tales
In the dark night, let me
Lie by your side, gaze
Lost in you

Lover

Linger in my thoughts
Just a little longer
Like your fingers around my neck
Just how I like it
Lower you shield
Just to let me in
Lumber into my domain
Just as I wander in yours
Longing to stay tethered
Just like I can't bear to be away long
Lapse time with no lament
Just like we do when tangled in the sheets

LOVE, LOSS & PEACE

I'm yours

Say my name all gentle like
Whisper in your dreams you love me
Hold me closer in the dim lit rooms
Lean in and let your breath fan my nape
For times when I'm in your arms
I dream of peaceful slumbers
Curled into a tangled pair
Hidden in alcoves only we know of
Sigh your wishes in my ear
Breathlessly plunder my nightmares
Waking my yearning spirit
Serene as it rises from the torment I lie in

NINA MTANU

Friendship

As we sat sipping tea
We shared the turbulent times we'd had
We laughed about the silly moments
We clasped hands about the loss
We embraced the sadness that lingered
We celbrated the milestones
We lamented what was out of reach
As the tea got cold, and
The night rolled in
Our secrets simmered into full shapes
We gathered our truths and spared none
The faith we had in each others strength
The budding respect of one another grew
As we sloshed remnants of tea
We leaned even closer
We embraced the yearning
We scampered over fear and roared
We ate ravenously at the banquet of love
We simmered the feelings of eternity's start

LOVE, LOSS & PEACE

...

Is it daylight?
If there has not been a star studded sky
Wishes blinking out of focus
Yearnings too loud in the silence
As the midnight sun casts our secrets
In the illumination of bottomless confessions
Bright night awakenings

Tell me

Tell me all of it
Bequeath me the truth of your devotion
Surrendered to its enormity
I wait for the cascade of your words
Desperate like the desert
So,
Tell me all of it
The words you whisper as I sleep
The thoughts that fleet by and you smile
The anguish that fills you that you detach
The hollow that lives in you, always taking
The commotion of happiness that grips you
The wishing that stays despite hopes low tide
The simplicity of our love that you write about
The courage it takes to not abandon this ship
The comfort to be so free in love
So,
Tell me all of it
Without stalled breaths I might leave
Without amoured approach and lie
Without the sadness of lost time

Selfish love

Those soulful bottomless eyes wide
Fingers lightly resting over mine
Breaths bated
The moment thrums with promise
As our bodies careen toward each other
Chins lifting
Still unsure but hopeful
I gaze at you
The softest petal touch to my rough edges
My selfishness knows no bounds
I'll keep you at my breast, hoard your love
As your gasp floats in the wind
Lashes falling over delicate cheeks
Poised with a silent need
I descend with care
Trembling at the touch of your lips on mine
To love and to hold
I drink from your kindness
Gentle and light unlike my jagged surface
My keeper of beasts with bleeding hearts

NINA MTANU

...

Your half-hearted words of denial
Are blunt scissors
To the red string of us
Stiching us close
Even in the silence

LOVE, LOSS & PEACE

No ordinary love

Rest me where the pillows are soft
Plumb with your whispers
And warm with your arms around me
Lay me on your heart
Tattooed by the unabashed adorations
I'll wear the marks like medals
Prints of your kisses on my collars
I long for you every second
Camped on snowy soft slopes
A love not ordinary
Lapping up the fall for you I sigh by the fireplace
Hearts fanned to full roar of an inferno

Featured in *Reigningwordsnyc* read up

NINA MTANU

Smiles and Grins

To hold such a beauty
The sight of your smile
Upon words I uttered,
I'm at home
Knowing you bequeathed me
Such a rare gem

All the kisses

Kiss me under the moonlight
Kiss me in the rain
Kiss me in the dark
Kiss me as the sun sets
Kiss me as the sun rises
Kiss me when elated
Kiss me when lost
Kiss me when unsure
Kiss me when we're lost
Kiss me under the stars
Kiss me under the hulking trees
Kiss me under water
Kiss me on the desert
Kiss me wounded
Kiss me in celebration
Kiss me in search of stilness
Kiss me during chaos
Kiss me in this spot we meet every night
Lay all your kisses at my feet and let me carry their weight with you

NINA MTANU

...

Will your tongue
Find space
Between my scars
To place hurt
Or soothe the aches

Wonder

Through the threads of reality
Sewn tight by routines
Starched stiff by rules
Draped enticingly on dollar bills
Stitched on folded dreams
Wrinkled by fatigue
And stained by rolling revolutions
You reach through
Thimble thin
Razor sharp
Pointed peak
Blinding light
Tearing my world apart
In ripping tears you stretch
My name on your soft lips you call
Guilded warrior you match into my war
Laden with balms on your tongue and touch
Your eyes adorn me with a love so pure
And words cascade with care so gentle
You're a magic wonder in this stark reality

Kiss

My heart flutters
As your fingers trace over my palm
Giddy smile and eyes wide
Your palm slides over mine
My bashful gaze cast to the side hastily
You twine our hands in the air
My gaze wanders back to your captive one
As you twist our hands from side to side
Patient and mirtful eyes roaming over me
You drape my dainty arm over your shoulder
My breath stalls, time slows
Tipping my chin up, you lose yourself in me
Mesmerised as we fall into each other
Searching lips parting a breaths away
Then we exhale upon the first touch

DESIRE

NINA MTANU

Fall

Low lidded gazes
Slow winding kisses
Soul stirring whispers
Warm running petting
Deep rumbling groaning
Life breathing coupling
Night ebbing slumbers
Low lighting ambers
Swift shooting biting
All drawn out loving
Late waking hours
Flight taking senses
Lulled smoudering feelings

Lovers gaze

Unfurl your feathers my love
Bare yourself and come undone
Shimmering under the golden hues
I wish to look at you
Unfazed and unabashed
As we clothe each other with only our eyes
Unrushed and unthehered on this night
We will bathe in each others sighs
Preening under whispered praises
Come to me darling
Fearless and ready
Declare your intentions as your hands roam
Lips all over my skin and mark me as yours
In this domain, we lay our fears at the door
Ferocious with our hunger for each other
We'll descend like silken swathes of heat
Clutched to my breast as we tumble and rise
Ordained in our brewed love
We'll soar in tandem
A pouring crescendo of euphoria

NINA MTANU

Devotion

Don't you see it?
As your eyes glaze over
Breaths coming in choppy gasps
Your nails raking paths on my flesh
Don't you hear the loud call of my reverence?
Don't you feel it?
Our restless bodies slapping
Words hummed amid grunts and moans
Your keens a spiral that propels us deeper
Don't you feel how much I've come to care?
Don't you see it?
As my hand circles your neck
Clamping around me in excitement
Your arching need to get closer to me
Don't you see how gone I am for you bared?
Don't you taste it?
Our savoured licks and nibbles
Tracing infinate lines over our souls
Your cradled flesh under my care
Don't you taste how unique our union is?

Lustful love

Ravenous,
Our hands skim and hold
Yearning,
Our bodies collide in a rush
Untamed,
Our lips slide and dip at angles
Unbriddled,
Our passion urges us on
Feverish,
Our breaths singe the stillness
Synchronised,
Our groans and moans echo
Shuffling
Our movement jerks us to a wall
Delirious,
We part to suck in breaths, grinning
Undulating,
The worshiping hums chorus
Creasting,
The raging tide of lust builds
Unleashed,
We tumble on floors unbothered
Carnal,
We chase the rolling tides life surfers
Unchained,
We rush the unexpected ventures
Depleated,
We slide under sheets naked
Sighing,
We relish the begining of us
Waking,

Kisses and cuddles melt the panic
Cocooned,
We laze amidst pitched tents
Entwined,
Our fingers point to stars aligned and clasped.

LOVE, LOSS & PEACE

...

Hike your desires
Like your breaths
Up my nape
Feverish wants
Like you're mine
Up all night

Drip

Drip
Onto my hands
Drip
On my skin
Drip
Into my mind
Drip
Onto my soul
Drip
Into my thoughts
Drip
Into my life
Drip
Into my strife
Drip
Into my pain
Drip
Into my love
Drip
On my flesh

Night owl

Part your blinds
Slide the sheets to the side
Glide on smooth pleats
Sigh my name
as I
Cart your wants
Grind the keens in the night
Pile on booth screams
High on game
as I
Craft your desires
Pound the beams on freight
File on booked calls
Eye on feign
as I
Depart you sleep

NINA MTANU

Riders

I won'tride you with difficulty
Like a mare unseasoned for my seat
But like a stallion at last calmed
I want to kiss your fingers
Suck on your skin
Trail the murmurs of devotion on your curves
Digging posts of reminders in enamel nibbles
Feel the dents of my fingertips
Decorated warrior my bruising love will show
Those legs on my shoulders incense potent
I will sink to my knees in reverence as I eat
It's leg day in leisure and I
Track your homage in pleasure
Featured in *Reigningwordsnyc* read up

Stars

Don't hold my love in
Open
Let my love run in you
Pearl tributaries cascades
As they fill every opening
Swallow
My might of a thousand stars
Burning hot and yours
Glow in my presence
Hum
As it runs over from the sides
Sodden lips and heart full
Embrace and bear the illumination

NINA MTANU

Tangled

You love this tangled mess we are
Under dimmed lights and sighs
We flutter like black moths
Chasing the whispers of love
And you my darling laid on the roses
Clad in your beautiful naked self
Begiled I've come under your guidance
So hear me out when I sing
My melodies
Hums of my devotion
As I tell you of how
I have succumbed

LOVE, LOSS & PEACE

Won't you be mine?

Won't you be mine?
With your beguiling words
And mesmersing dark eyes
Won't you be mine?
With that intriguing voice
And spellbinding movements
Won't you be mine?
With your unforgettable wit
And perched in my thoughts every second
Won't you be mine?
With your relentess hide and seek
And unabashed sensuality
Won't you be mine?
With your endless bespelled stories
And unhurried gait
Won't you be mine?
Witholding nothing this night
And plunge me into a night of debuchery
Won't you be mine?
With your bashful smile
And gaze that holds true

...

They think
Your desires set where your robes fall
But I've lifted the linings of your dress
Kissed the long miles to reach
Cascading water bodies
That serve delicacies special
Slumbered on canyons and woken
To moaning sunrises
Veiled in silk murmurs and divan bossoms

Choker

By all means
Wear my digits caress
Choker necklace behind doors
Simmer to a boil as I watch on
Breaths fast and moans low
As eyes dip to setting suns
Bodies slap cheers
Intervals of 3 2 1
We come

NINA MTANU

In the night

Why don't you flip that cocoa cascade over?
Spread the sighs over the long hours,
Hitch the keens higher past my ears
Glide those ankles over high peaks,
Let your words arch into the right dip
Wider, push the range of my stamina
Applause as the chase grows rough
Take all, as ravenous hunger takes us over
Harmonies as breaths litter the room,
Jiggles all over as cups spill over
Clutch whimpers over creasing sheets,
Swallow as rods tighten around your neck
Braids reins, ride the stallion mound
Full of steam, blow hard
Tetonic treamors unending profess your love

Long nights

Rolling tides to top rides
Claps and bounce
Long nights
Pulling grips to deep slides
Hands and groans
Hold tight
Pooling rips to pop bursts
Laps and sips
First rounds
Growing nips to deep sucks
Chokes and kisses
Good girls

Sip with moderation

How should I enjoy you?
Quick like a flaming tequila shot?
Blazing through my veins and heart
And just as we enjoy the bitter-sweetness
You are gone from my arms
My thoughts scrambled and bitter
And yet I yearn for one more shot
How should I enjoy you?
Like a mellow red, glass half full?
Sharp you waltz into my life
And you stay as I rearrange things to fit
You fill every crevice of my life
With your well rounded essence and ease
But a niggling part reminds me
You are not mellow every time
This love brews to sour if we fail
How should I enjoy you?
Like a spirit's hard or smokey allure?
Your quick wit and firey tongue lures me in
Your femme-fatale begiling sway zings
As your charm warms me
Your then sheathed claws leave memoirs
Our short lived pounding menace burns
Clincking around my mind as your face swirls
How should I enjoy you?
Like a cocktail mix?
One moment we make love
We bathe in the sacred waters of oneness
Soon we're heated
Cursing tongues and flailing hand gestures
You drive me to brink of euphoria

And I shimmy as I sip your nectar endlessly
Doomed I love you, wicked but wounded
How should I enjoy you?
Bitter and sharp like caffine?
I sit by the window and billow my distate
Agony over my loss of you sits near
I remember the aroma of your laugh
Your smiles were artworks of your feelings
The days you shed your masks and lay bare
The nights and winters you mixed in trends
I frantically search my memories of your face
How should I enjoy you?
With milk or clear like my tea?
Calming you hum and my nerves settle
I feel the drape of your being all over
Cradled in your sweetness and bites
I clutch you to me and close my eyes
Even as you scald when you get clingy
I rest my head on your chest and you lull me
Your soft wafting voice sings me to sleep
How should I enjoy you?
Clear of worries like the water in my cup?
How you stay put as I try to find myself
You carry burdens with ease and I heave
Cascading over my misery, you cleanse
At a standstill, you wrench my traumas out
Galavanised by your quiet ebb I let go
Trickling into hollows filled with dread
I sip and weep as your clarity eludes me now

NINA MTANU

...

Lips inches apart
Gasping in tremors
Gripped with need
The air is fresh
Heated exhales

Innuendos

Through veiled words
You sneak
Through barely gaping curtains
You sway
Through illuminating low lights
You dance
Through loaded songs
You speak
Through dusky silhouettes
You sway
Heaping drops you feign into my thoughts
Through hummed laughs
You cajole
Through slightly ajar doors
You entice
Through gaping pages
You whisper
Through light grazes
You simmer in my veins
Through passing glances
You remain a fixture
Mounting primed need onto spilling cups

Sex

This endless rupture
Bountless curves of soft brown
Spread over my shuddering praises
Under rippling tides of keens
Your touch ignites
Inciting rallies that roar
Selfless service that seeks climatic peaks
Dazed cheers cascade down heated flesh
Glistening desire stewed in pants
Licking grunts moan a symphony
Rising mounds and slapping joys
Tonight we bathe in sex
Glued to stitch this burning love
A rumbling crest and naughty asks

Pearls

Traversing silken slopes
Dipping high and low
My thumb goes
Overseeing the open space
Curious to caress every spot
Your breaths patter under my touch
Massaging circles over pearl smooth skin
I wander unrestricted
Curving out the edges of your jaw
Smoothing hollows over your chin
My desire pours out in fevered breaths
Pressing the warmth of you to me
The lines of your lips call out
Soft pillows laden with promise
I rub softly
Parting folds that heave with heat
I tumble in
Welcomed by the slippery insides
Your shy tongue licks my thumb
Sharp teeth grazing and I shudder

NINA MTANU

Sermon

Your body is my altar
Where I lay my confessions
A reverence of litanies uncorked
Let me annoint your skin with the ink
Of my devotion
Humming with pleads
As I
Pluck the strings between your peaks
Conducted by sensations to sate
Choirs of harmonies reign in our chambers
Sing me to soars
And I
Follow line by line to your heart
Spread on my lectern my sermon divine
Pearls commune to swallow chastity

Part 2

HEART BREAK

Heart ache

Don't offer broken promises
Discarding broken glass
Down the craters of my chest
Let me languish in woe
Bemoaning my haste feelings
Cast off to shore and burnt
The willowy wails of the wind my lullaby

Fallen Cities

Through the unseen crevices of that love
The sharp words we exchanged, prickly
The dented edges of once plump adoration
The crumbling bricks of regrets
Whistling wails echoes
The scattered stones of careless jabs
The sour yearning of apology, trips my tongue
Thimbles of spite and complains piled
Totaled grounds lay abandoned
The woeful cries of a fallen city of love
Hearts hum as they trudge on in sadness
Blood slow with heavy intentions
Rued encounters and confused lone nights
Buried sighs and rumbling smothered laughs
Homed in tombs visible through dull eyes
Troubled waters flood the eyes and stall
Wet words filled with smothered screams
Scorched and left in shambles is the fallen city of a once great love

LOVE, LOSS & PEACE

Fast love

Euphoric seconds morph
Into minutes as we kissed
Hours passed under moonlit skies
We spend days planning alternate future
Months swelled with our anticipated futures
Years span in looping laps of change
And yet, the albums at my feet are all I have
Memories shaded in grey
You echo in hazy glimmers like a dream
Do I remember you or I read a book?
Filled with sorrow of a fast love
Delirium brimming that we ignored
The signs and flew past broken gates
Is it your lullaby that I doze off to
Or do I imagine who you'd be as I wait?

Regret

Sitting on these sunken cushions
Bones heavy
Tongues heavy
Hearts heavy
Breaths wispy
We wish we said what we felt
Sitting in this vast room
Lips trembling
Eyes scouring
Lungs labouring
Fists tightening
The regret of our silence drips

LOVE, LOSS & PEACE

...

I thought words could
Quell this strorm
But the ink pours turbulent
Like the wildness in my mind
The downpour on my cheeks endless

Bottled time

These delicate vases
Laden with so much
Dread
Grief
Regret
Fear
These clear glasses
Laden with so much
Longing
Confusion
Stagnation
Defeat
These bottled feelings
Laden with so much of
Yesterday
Last time
Years ago
Previously
These stacked crates
Laden with so much of
I'm sorry
I wish
If only
It's too late
These feelings swirl in bottles on the shelves of my decisions
Changing colours that mesmerise
I'm a dealer who sells because they won't change back time

Heartbreak

Lying here as my heart tears
Like cracking canoyns
Thoughts broken pieces
Scattered love crashing around me
Crushing realisations of finality loom
I feel the clench of rising cries in my throat
My eyes burn with scalding regrets
Swimming in gurgled apologies
I shake in the cold spot by the floor
The moorings of pride creak
The creasting hurt and denial, a tug of war
Where do I stash this buckling rage?
This crippling pain that weakens me?
But loss knows no prior serenity
It burges in, tidal waves slithering everywhere
It uproots every promise, every sure thing
Savage in its thourough eradication
And I cling to sanity as my reality shifts
I'm no longer who I was
This new hollow place will be part of me
Jagged and scarred and full of doubts

NINA MTANU

Loving a 'Tough' man

Bared, my fears bleed into the silent room
With trembling words
I beg for love
My mind loud as my insecurities flare
But his stoic front reflects my efforts
This house reeks of withered love
Like dried roses I prop up our vain unity daily
To love a tough man despite it all
His shaking hands cluth his words
His bobbing vocals heavy with their weight
My watery eyes implore him to open up
With a shaking hand I clutch his
Lost, but volatile I watch my lover sink
Suspending us in this shrivelled pit where love's hope dooms us every minute
But I persist
Trying to pry the scar over his heart until he bleeds with me
Clutched to me as I teach him to love
But tonight, we sleep defeated
Again, I doubt not leaving

...

Open, my waters
You sipped
Vanishing,
Alone I sit
Ice cold
To thaw for another

NINA MTANU

I never loved you

I never loved you
And not because I want to hurt you
But I lied to myself
Day and night
I watched your eyes adorn me with curiosity
I watched your eyes adorn me with intrigue
I watched your eyes adorn me with unease
I watched your eyes adorn me with love
I watched your eyes swim with confusion
I never loved you
And not because I want to hurt you
But I convinced myself
Seasons and moments
I listened as you lay your secrets bare
I listened as you fumbled with emotions
I listened as you bravely declared to love me
I listened as you tore at your pain and grew
I listened as you skirted around us
I never loved you
And not because I mean to skewer you
But I've been lying to myself
Days and years
I've been a failure at letting you go
I've been too cruel thinking I have it in me
I've been a trickster because I gave you none
I've been barren of love all this time
I've been too selfish and gobbled you up
I never loved you
And not because I mean to hurt you
But I've never opened that pandoras box
I've been the thief of your time and I'm ashamed

Ignited

That feverish love of ours
It burned me so hard
Yet I danced in it
I lay in the flames of your lust
Covered in melted sinful whispers
And I'd do it again
To be ignited so wholly

NINA MTANU

Let me break

I can be strong
I can be there to hold
I can stay by you in storms
But let me break
When it gets too much
And tears well in my eyes
Do not stop me
Do not forbid me
Do not remind me
That I should be strong
Refuse to see we weep and deny me
Don't demand that I not be weak then

LOVE, LOSS & PEACE

...

When you leave
Make sure
The door is not ajar
Close up and let me stew in it
Suffocating in the finality
Of your depature
Your words etched on my skin
The arrows of my words
Piled on my tongue
Don't leave me a chance of vindicaion
I don't know to hunt the light
Or chase after you in oblivion
For one more taste even in shame at my weakness

NINA MTANU

Frigid hearts

Cradling these fragile
beats,
Thrums of life, you
know nothing
Frigid, you bleed
cynic

Do you see?

Do you see?
The strings stitching the smile
As my glassy eyes crease
And my trembling hands clutched stiff
Do you see?
The falling pieces scattered lines
As my breathless words shutter out
And the lie pours out
Do you see?
As my shoulders tremble under boulders
And my ramrod spine tries to stay
As my world erodes
Do you see?
I hide under the illusion the strength
As my waning conviction hangs by a breath
And I swallow all the wails and tears
Do you see?
The calls for help hanging on my neck
Thundering through thickets of wallows
And I heave each morning
Do you see me, disappearing?

NINA MTANU

Her

At times her
Emotions rose so high
And I was always in awe of,
The beauty of her expressions
Turbulent, you
Stay
Harrowed by this present, culminating
A presence so deep, that
I
Ache to be close to you
A mythical being, made
Of the mosaics of your experiences
Tenured by your conviction, to
Not quit even as the burden grows

...

When flowers die
Hearts too sigh
Withered in contempt
Doused in defeat
When lovers lie
Beloveds do cry
Bygone illusions

NINA MTANU

Bygone youth

Even when I felt the weight of life
I never imagined
I'd sit here on the porch staring off and lost
That I'd put on a smile while I crumbled
Shivering in the cold wake of our divorce
Alone, the future stretches
The echoes of our love a faint beat
Even when I thought to bargain
I never imagined
I'd cry myself to sleep
The void of our united front throbs
All the milestones I've birthed and nurtured
I lag behind as he moves on
Planted in this abyss of ache and tears
Even when I felt our love invincible
I never imagined
Being the bereft one who got the pitying looks
Withered and washed up
Splattering tears tapping a rhythmic sad song

Stay

These endless tears
They stain my nights
Unbidden they slip
Overflowing and flooding
I beg the winds to dry them
But I plummet further
Entombed in your departure
Their presence reeks of finality
Loots of wars

Lost love

Your feet, wading
The waters
My face, lay submerged
As the slosh of your
Progress to leave filled my ears
I, lay mute
As the water boyed, my
Broken heart swimming
In my emotions

...

Do you search for me in the crowd?
Eyes eager
Breaths bated
Mind churning
Or have you forgotten
Locked me up with
The rest of your pain

NINA MTANU

Knowing

Don't catch me
With oil slicked fingers
Only for me to fall further
Let me plummet
Petrified of the fate that awaits
Aware of all the pain
Because in your arms
I'm suspended in fear of falling
Shrouded in disappointment dressed as care

Wrong lanes

There have been so many
You bared yourself to
Who still never saw
Your face of pure bliss

Toxic

We were forged in the same fire
Run red hot and capable
Yet we couldn't be further apart
Your cold ways that keep you detached
I have lingered closer trying to warm you
But your blizzard chills my inferno
Brutal in your enduring mantra
And I burn to thaw what died in you
Caramelise your essence that other flock
I crackle with desire to wake your dormant love
Forbidden, you stay aloof
And I blow close to you snuffed by your icicles
And I still burn

...

If I could
I'd reach for you
Even denied
To ask you one last time
Had I done right?
Was I ready?
And yet I stall
Where did I hide my courage

Lured

My dignity stripped off hapazardly
Your eyes sting my raked over pride
You gathered your tools
Lubricated my shield with lies
When I began to chip and crack
You lay in wait
Claws ready
As you herded me forth
Bound for a ravenous crowd's entertainment
You shot your daggers
Paralysed in place
Snared and wounded
I writhed
As your showmanship gannered more roars
Your words all along rang true
I'd been deceived
Doused in false pretenses of affection
Drowsy from constant confusion
Your talons gouged until I rang hollow
Fodder for your destruction

Thief

You took
My voice and hid my words
You took
My dreams and hid my plans
You took
My days and hid my nights
You took
My silence and hid my calm
You took
My sound and hid my strum
You took
My past and hid my feelings
You took
My heart and hid my beats
By book
You played and hit the mark
By book
You slayed and hit the gold
By book
You stole and hid my life

NINA MTANU

...

Will my denial
Eclipse the yearning
Scattering whims to nothing
Silence,
My bed fellow

Ends

Even beautiful things die
Some a quick death
Some a painful death
Some a tortured death
All in all, it all comes to an end

Collision

This longing that never wanes
The moons diary is full of my secrets
About you
The times when I call out
I promise I will wait
For you
And I wake to silence
What if we never collided?
One of two
Spread apart in parallels
Would the room be full or empty?
With doom

Beautiful tragedies

Like fireflies, that smile got me
Carefree and mooning
Like night stars, that voice had me
Reeled in and hanging for more
Like butterflies, that exuberance endeared me
Opening my shut heart wide open
Like eager eyes, that lightness consumed me
Snapping off the chains around my body
Like sniper aims, those words revived me
Breathing newness into my exhausted soul
Like glitter winks, the stolen moments flew
Snapshots of loves whirlwind
Soft touches and wild nights
Summer laughs and winter clutches
Swift thunderstorms and raining kisses
Turbulent whisperes and plummeting sighs
The beautiful tragedy that befell our love
The chaos synchronised in thorny harmonies

NINA MTANU

...

Gather all the olive branches
I send
Siphon the kindness from them
And write me
Letters inked in their oils
Laden with my echoes
My hearts fireplace
Awaits kindling

Eternal

Pick up one of the pieces
And you'll find
Your name on it
Scattered all over this floor
In these broken pieces
I still cradle you close
Scared of letting you go
And even when I stitch them back
I will feel the scribble of your name
Lining every part of me for eternity

Burning star

I'm not your salvation
I'm a burning star
Illuminated in its flames
As it burns
Its last resort of being memorable
My glimmering rays are what fools you
But soon I'll take you with me
Into a dark oblivion that sucks in matter
Run and save yourself
There's not bright future here
But a yawning dark endless pit
Spin out of my galaxy and shine bright
My journey is but a beat race
And I don't want you to burn out too

Steady love

My hands offer these soft petals of adoration
Cast in hues of
Understanding
Wit
Peace
Slow pace
Tranquiliy
Chasing beats as we change turns and tides
But you, laden with your labours
Keep trampling on them
Crunching colours under your boots
Crying blindness
When I know even deaf you'd know
And this is what you call steady love
But I have grown weary
Pouring from a cup that is running empty
And you sip like a dried well syphoning
Thirsting to revive but cost the ecosystem
These petals wilt at your door
But will thrive elsewhere
Featured in **Reigningwordsnyc** read up

Shedding

Dripping
Your lips glistened
With my blood
Vindicated
As I lay gasping
My secrets exposed
Humiliated
Wincing from the pain
Cut core deep
I vowed
To bleed you out
Your existance wiped off
Stitched
I whimpered in silence
Reborn and scarred
Certain
I willed to live
Removed from perfected lies

LOVE, LOSS & PEACE

...

Rain drops falling
Your shade a gloom
You dug
Chipping my roots
Killing me

THE FURY OF HEALING

Healing

In this life
I too have been unkind
When my heart has been so torn
Shredded and discarded
I have slain others as I fought
To gather the pieces
Some lost forever
And others too scarred
In the healing that came after
I have realised
That in this life
I have not been gentle at times
And I have sat with my callous words
Chocked on the pain they caused
Wracked with guilt
And I have lain in agony
Slain by the words of others
And I chose to be kind
To pet the feathers I've ruffled
Swallowing the bitter with the sweet
Vibrant in the ascend of acceptance

Gaping pain

As you spoke
You reeked of it
The sharp barbs
Told of pains cling
You wrestled with it
But with ease it stayed
Harnessing all the positive
Borrowing all of your strength
Leaving you hollow and wallowing
Barrelling towards distaste and anguish
As you stood helpess but in hiding
You oozed its poisonous stench
The defeated eyes and spirit
Spoke of the times warp
And you still fought
Bargaining with it
Refusing to sit
Defiling theft
Despite loss
Healing

Stillness

Even when I might want to rampage
I choose to sit still
To hear my loud thoughts
To peer into the mayhem roiling within me
To refuse the rattling chains snare
To ease my mind by emptying the chuff

Dearly departed

You confuse me with
Someone kind
I am not
When I was a child
I killed those parts of me
I rioted before their doors
I sang songs of impending doom
And when they were most vulnerable, I struck
I slit their throats
I relished their cries
I bathed in ther blood
The aftermath,
A husk of my former self
Callous
Brutal
Detached
Leeched of love
And sun dried of softness
So don't look into my eyes
And search for a gentle love
Becasue you won't find it on these shores
The sand of my dried tears will sting you
So board your ships and sail to better shores

Parts of you

There was a part of you
That wanted to strip me of myself
There was a ravenous part of you
That seethed knowing I stood tall
There was a part of you
That tried and tried again
To shutter my windows with heavy blinds
There was a part of you that yearned
To quickly squash my words
There was a part of you
That was feral and fed on decay
There were so many times
That I loathed your bullish manner
There was a part of you
That I could never be close to, so I left

Bruisers

I carry these wounds with me
Some healed scars
Others filled with raw phantom agonies
And when I remember the times
I sit with them
They've molded me into a fighter
Bruised but deadly
For every drop of blood
I too will swipe for a spray

Abuse

Even when the body heals
Abuse does not leave the mind
The memory of the swipe of your hand
The manic look in your eyes as you neared
The bared teeth as you exacted your feelings
Even when the body heals
Abuse does not leave the mind
The taste to copper in the mouth
The rattling of bones as my body readied
The crumbling of my bravery as you neared
Even when the body heals
Abuse does not leave the mind
The constant verbal battering
The unpredictable swing of moods
The thick fog of being hunted and powerless
Even when the body heals
Abuse does not leave the mind
The times I failed myself in guilt
The shame I carry remembering captivity
The paralysis that grips me to know you live

Letting go

Your time too came
Your moments passed
Your luster faded
Your words grew rusted
And I watched them dissolve
And I sat with the finality of it
And I let the lingering hurt settle
And I grew to be strong again
It was just a season
It was a learning curve
It was a growing phase
It was a needed change
For I too were once naive
For I too wanted it all
For I too had time
For I needed to be taught
You were a page stretched into a chapter, riddled with vagabond tendancies under the guise of a future

Spoils

Every war
Has its spoils
I like to keep mine
To remind me of the time I lost
To remember the energy I gave away

Rued

Rue me
Vow to you
Enchanted you dance
Rue me
Believe in you
Protected you match
Rue me
Bow to you
Disbanded you're free
Rue me
Say to you
'Armoured' you're a lethal blade
Rue me
Choice is you
Ride into the wild of your dreams

Light hunters

You hunt stars
Weaving through milky ways
Gleeful as their shimmer lands on your palm
You've filled your house with them
Blinding bright you walk into the night
And yet you still hunt
Never satiated
Salivating
Galavanting
The night you left in me
Watches on, gentle and learning
I glow in this abyss too
Shimmers of blue black mesmerising
Hang your bows and count your luck

NINA MTANU

Burn

Burn
An inferno of feelings
Streaming out in heavy words
Dream this reality into a state of end
Delirium crowding like a ravenous beast
A heathen amongst your thoughts of perfect
Burn
This tedium of repeats
Strip the bare bars of your essence
Cast it in the pit of reflective boredem
Filled with writhe as the culmination grows
Ripping the waves tumble as the truth rolls out
Burn
The lies you grip
Tethered to your fears
Slang over the creaking edge
Splinter into a million pieces and vanish

Aftermath

I've tasted nothing worse
Than the watered down parts of me
The pitiful sloshing of values
Cascading down kettle mouths badly spiced
The paling taste sticking to my throat
I curl words laden with lead
My worksmith field cluttered with sadness
Dull blades slumber behind my lips
Sharpening anvils long abandoned

NINA MTANU

Dust in the wind

I stopped carrying you around
The weight of your callous words
The sight of the other side of your being
The disgust that covered my thoughts
I rid my house of your reek
I bathed and emerged feather light
Like dust in the wind
I dusted you off my eyes window sills
I cast open all crevices
I tipped all tear filled cups out the house
I erased the traces of your disrespect
My home now blooms care and calm
I tend to love and support and bask in growth

Rehersal

These words sit on my tongue like lead
Coalesced from the thick guilt within
And I let them roll around
Cresting and gannering momentum
And I still sit
These words pour out of my lips with vinegar
Acrid and sharp from the churning
And I let them fly like darts
Pinpointing my target like a hunter
And I still speak
These actions bolster my vindication
Turbulent and heaving from a charge up
And I dare not stay still
Pushing a boulder with a might of a beatle
And I still stare at the mirror

Rebirth

I don't seek reverence at your foot
I don't need to feel alive by your adoration
Exorcising of my demons needs me alert
Ready and determined every second
As I fall my limbs fill with vigor
Efforts brimming with hindsight
To repeat my agonies over and over
And still find my resovle unwavering
Don't clutch me to you to stall
I'll run into the wilds of my trauma and fight
Resilient and angered to have been robbed
Plucking at the lump at my throat holding in secrets
Hurling them from my flesh like tumours
Tearing open the doors where pain rattles inside
Menancing and fed up I glare at it
Prepared by years of simmering anger
Slicing at the orderly state of its existance
And watch it cascade
Down my skin in glittering drops
Cutting the closing wounds again and again
Letting the poison of habits drip from my mind
Heaving every second I renounce my cycles
Bathed in the crimson of my pasts chains
Reborn into a beast without a cage
Roaming the plains of existance anew
Life brims at the foot of the falls depths

LOVE, LOSS & PEACE

Passing Storms

Sometimes,
My chest gapes
And all there is,
Is salt to rub on it
I grit my teeth
Hold in the wail
Bathing my cheeks in warm rivers
And when I can breathe again
I let out the screams

NINA MTANU

Perfect

Everyone wants perfection
Glazed tops
Straight lines
Starched tops
Sharp points
Smooth coats
In the wake of slumped backs
Jagged roads
Thorny corners
Lumpy seats
Sunken promises
Everyone wants perfection
Glittering tops
Meadow breezes
Standing ovations
Bowed heads
Simpering agreeables
In the wake of bygone respect
Callous tones
Thrashed patience
Strangled zen
Charred unity
Rag dolled individuality
Everyone wants perfection
An elusive entity
Smokescreen projection
A void existance

Call my name

Reach me
In these deep depths of despair
Say my name even as I hide
Echoes of your louding voice unrelenting
Chase my sinking form and grasp
I've held on so long and efforts grew limp
Reach me
In the abyss

NINA MTANU

Old pages

It is too late now
For gestures
For words
For time
That chapter closed
That period passed
That naivety died
So let me go

Masquerade

Even when they ask for all the truth
Most people want to hear the lies
In the quiet dead of the night
When we whisper about life
People want to pretend.
I tell the truth
Too beautiful
Too painful
No remorse
After,
I sit alone when you've fled

NINA MTANU

Moving on

And when I grew wiser
I hang up the dancing shoes
Feet bruised and bloody
Heart battered
Mind delirious
Thoughts heavy
Soul scarred
Skin drenched
Your contamination pungent
I wept
For the naive girl
Who gave too much
For the countless times
I hoped again and fell flat

LOVE, LOSS & PEACE

You'd be … years today

Sometimes we wait
Lying low like loss hasn't come
Swept in its upchuck of mayhem
We float in the petrification of shock
And we wait
For the signal to go
But days pass by slow
Months soon become years
Caught in the fray of bargaining
But we miss
The chapters opening
Riffling new pages that await
Laden with promise of new smiles
Because we've been preoccupied at the port

Grieving

Grieving is only shared deeply behind doors
Outsiders meet your strong facade with pity
But they hear not, the
Frustrated screams, the
Unyielding eyes of sorrow,
Glazed over with resentment
Outsiders are not privy to the,
Wishes of getting back what you lost
They never hear of the whimpers
The bargaining wails
The pounding of walls and floors
See the defeated slide downs on shaky legs
Outsiders see a courageous person moving on
But the crumbled insides topple at home
Hidden in beak rooms full of stale air
Stiffling memories, and
Unyielding realites
Briming with resentment, and
Choking with uncertain futures
Outsiders, never see journals full of anger
Stumbling upon sad words strung together
Scribbled sorries that 'I lived and they died'
Heavy letters that weigh the ink onto creaking lines

Grief

When you have loved and lost
Sit with the pain
Wallow in the grief
Plunge into the loss
And then slowly begin to wash off in time
As the ebbing tide begins healing the void
Allow yourself to accept it
Breaking down at odd times
Don't deny the emptiness left
Even when your eyes fill as you laugh
Carry that loved one in your words
Thoughts heavy, throat clogged suddenly
Cry as you laugh
Clutch them to you even as you set them free
To love is a gift
To let life move on, is a lesson

NINA MTANU

Loss teaches

I've carried it around for years
Laden with its sudden presence
It has weighed on me when I wanted to fly
I have laughed and felt it choke me
I have searched for ways to ease it
And yet, grief stayed
I wandered into all places trying
I looked in different places wishing
I let my heart lose hope crying
Until it whispered that I let grief in
I have laid here and wept
I have gone days bereft of sound
I have allowed myself the judgement
I have stayed silent with my guilt
I have swarm in the turbulent waters begging
And then it unfurled
Stretching and spreading
Like granules of rich soil it fell all over me
Renewed, I let it colour parts of me
Branded some of my memories with sadness
And I am whole, sad and happy

Desolate

Your pain,
When it took root
It opened its mouth
And in its clutches my innocence went
It gripped my mind so hard I trembled
My tongue shivered before I spoke
Words tumbled and vanished many times
I walked down these halls
Cradling my peace like a stolen token
I tiptoed around the hot coals
That rolled down your lips and singed
Yielding under the blade of your sorrow
Barbaric in it untamed strike
My room lay littered with whimpers
The destitute refuge camp
Where I stitched my punctured heart
Day and night
The needles' tip blunt with overuse
And I still wait
Hoping you will wean off the despair

NINA MTANU

The whisper

I carried you
In my mouth, for years
Like a dull rusted blade with
Serated edges
The shame of my actions
Cut now and then
I walked the streets
Wondering how I did that then
And your name grew heavier
On my tongue
Eroding my enamel
Stinging my gums
And I still kept on
Wondering how could I
Have done that then
And then I broke
My jaws too heavy
Words jumbled and bitter
Wilting ambtions sour
So I opened my lips
Letting brew dribble by
The blood from my bitten tongue
Curdled with your vile admonitions
Stayed with fears to speak up
And my jaw opened wider
Gurgling free
Throat expelling
The wrath of your disrespect
For days I sat
Months passed as I poured
And when the pooling poison began

To flow away from me
I let my mouth hang open
Calling forth,
Only a whsiper of my lions roar remained
And I smiled
I'd rid the anchor of you from my larynx
Paving the way for the gentle
Voice left
I'd roar again
Today, I was celebrating my voice

Alone

I'm an island
Savaged by the crashing
Words
Of your mouth
At times flocked to
Covered in a sea of chaotic praise
But soon
Like a passing season they
Fly away
Left barren and dry
Edges sharp and exposed
Shivering at the brace of the next wave

LOVE, LOSS & PEACE

Trauma bonds

The trauma bond
Was laden with
The past hurts
But bore no
Present
Carrying
Only
Future
Omens

Broken house

You were eager
To fall into this broken house
So sure you'd love me
When I told you
All the things I've done
Then your eyes shuttred
So I walked back into the broken house
Where I don't wait for one to see

After-taste

I think of you
And I'm filled with disappointment
You held so much potential
And yet you squader it
Don't begrudge my depature
Your comfort in fatigue grew tiresome

NINA MTANU

Cutting ties

You keep calling me
Coercing me to walk back in
But I ran to the woods
And wander through the thickets
Wailing and letting go of the suffocation
The air frees me as I trip over exposed roots
Although your echo chases me through the mist
Slithering through the canopies of growth
So I ask of you
Please, let me go
Wailing into the night and leave the misery
Because in here, the birds answer my cries
Bathing in the clear river water that calms me
So I ask of you
Please, don't write me and wait that I return
I closed the doors and threw the keys
I lost your self-made maps
Tore to shreads your deceit
And scream for the return of my freedom

Recluse

I've had my chaos
Run through the house of life
Trying to pry doors open
Petrified of never finding peace
I banged my hands raw and only locks jiggled
I exhausted my spirit enduring
So,
Let me live in calm
In this small place at the edge of it
Under the drooping canopies over the roof
Tittering birds flocking to my doorsep
River water trickling down steps away
Rustling leaves my siesta lullaby
Please,
Let me live in peace
Lost in the pages of the books
Crackling fire illuminating my nights
Whistling wind and humming leaves singing
Staring out from my perch unhurried
Smoke's signal my visibility from up the hill
Don't,
Disturb my peace

NINA MTANU

The fiddler

I've heard your violin play
A sleek perfomance, I was intrigued
Your pitch masquerading harmoniously
And yet as the melody wore on
I heard them,
The high pitched denials of your lies
The strings tied tight around your ex's freedom
Wobbling truth between the fast notes
And yet the symphony regaled
I gaped alarmed,
Heart pounding discovering sheets of facts
Conducted by your malice they begged off
But your personality bows only to your play

LOVE, LOSS & PEACE

Tragic love

It was a tragic love
Full of remiscent lulls
Glorious in its exposure of our darks
Delicate where it lay cradled in our fear
Blinding light where we accpeted each other
And then it burst
Flattering in haphazard spins of expectations
Startling the rest we'd fallen into
And it soared, unbeknownst to the sun
The feathers scattered as our union burned
Sooty wax smeared over laughs and mellows
Cascading down as the tears fell
It echoed in begged sniffles
Slipping off our hands as we grew distant
I have not loved like that again
So bare and courageous
Wounded so deep the pain wallows daily

Wild

I refuse to wither
In this well lit room
Filled with filtered air
Crackling stuffy hot fires
But my vines, have outgrown
The curved corners of your politeness
My roots reach and find no give in
The confines of your clutches
My sweated out leaves droop
I plot every night
I will grow
Outside
Wild

My scars

Would you kiss my scars?
As they lie exposed and glaring
Or do you only ever wish to see them
Staring through dulled eyes and hushed voices
Illusions of calm because storms scare you
Do you fear to see my scars?
As they endure and look impure
Or do you wish for my clothes to cover
Stiling yourself until their sight vanishes fast
Entombed bunkers of a battalions spirit
Because the groves of their lines remind me
Braille of my past paths lost road trips
I read them in the dark and sigh
They've led me home to rest
They've warned me
Of traitors

My dignity

Shame is the luxury of my dignity
To sell the very core of my values
To debase myself for just your gains
I'd be left at the doorstep begging for scraps
And I won't ever feed on those and be full
I will run down the hallways of hollowed fame
And I will beg every minute
Counting down the seconds
And when you've all had me
I will be cast off to the side
With no clothing of morals
And you will say I liked it
That I enjoyed the easy
That there was joy
But really it was
A transaction
Whose fine
Print was
Muddier

Sparks

Fear not the sparks of my fire
You think me too wild
Feral with an untamed will
But I won't exnguish my flames
Dim my voice so you slither over me
Watch on, begiled by my light
A star burning with no apology
For when I burn out and implode
I will take my joy in this wildness I live
A keepsake in the dark tunnels
Hurtling though voids and collecting chaos

...

You wanted a house full of kids
And a big wedding
And I wanted a companion
Renegades running from this mundane
I wanted a wild horse at heart
But you want the things that tie me up
Stiffled and stripped of my being
When I want the wild air on my face
So we buried that convoluted thought
And when it sprung up, an anthrax of laments
We parted bloody because, are we meant to be?

Veterans
Those who were there
During the war
Remember painful things
They see painful scenes
But are never believed
And those who arrived much later
Deny the sight ever being desolate
When the greenery has taken over
The air has grown fresh and free
Those who slept in gas masks stay quiet

Soar

From the clutches of settling
I soar at a night rider's speed
Bequeathed with the luck of second chance
My trembling voice grows form in the air
I soar in a spiral aiming to punture high
Snuggled in the breast of my fate
My grateful litanies emulate symphonies
I soar in the break of dawn
Birthed in the bloody aftermath of release
My quivering bones harden to stilts
I soar to glide in the wind
Unfamilliar with the uneven ground
My ever changing stasis unrelenting
I soar in a calm lift
Back arched, limbs loose, in fresh chilly air
My being inhales
I soar to burn your wax off my feathers

LOVE, LOSS & PEACE

Healing person

When you're touted as a 'good person',
You're not expected to have flaws
When you say, 'you're healing'
You may embody the image of 'a good person'
But you are never allowed to be flawed
Flaws are our bad habits
That helped us cope when we needed to
That gave us strength for a period
That helped us endure scarcity
To be healing, is not to be wholly renowed
To be healing , it's exorcising those habits daily
To be healing, is to burge into the den of tormentors
And as you get closer, you will see unhealed parts
That does not mean we wear masks
Healing takes the rest of our lives
To untangle the mess of life
To undo the mess of trauma
We're not, 'a good person'
We are a wounded person, nursing wounds
Purging the puss of habits
Willing to live with the scars

...

We talk in memories
Murals that flash and overwhelm
Like nothern lights
Beckoning me nightly
Still, tethered strangers

Lones

Friendships
Relationships
They all scare me
The expectations
Looming unknowns
I've only ever known myself
Been the closest person to confide in
So the unexpected length of a friendship
Cripples me with the fear of,
Maybe
I will fail the others
Unable to hold up
Incompetent
And I will
Disappoint
Accidentally wound others,
So
I tend to fall off
Led astray by my fears
A lone wolf content, but in need
Of company
Bonds I still fail to nutrure to maturity

Longing

My anger isn't graceful
I've wished I tsked when I remember
I've wanted to be inwardly seething
But the riot of my feelings
Overwhelms the resting shores of my lips
Breaching the dunes with flaming words
Your name tumbles out in flight
In pursuit my lament homes in on you
Berating your very existance in my life
'I wish I never met you'
I whisper sometimes
Breathed fire onto nails I hammer my lips
And yet you still find a way to slip out
I've laid down and stared into the night
Whispers of your name my comfort
But I burn in this roiling pit of longing
Damp with tears that drip occassionally
I loathe you and claim to love you in the same breath
Because there are parts
Parts of you that brought me peace during chaos
I know how kind you are
I remember I found solace in your silence
Your ego though, lay in wait
Growling, belly rumbling and you scorched me
Burned parts of my trust in you
Tattered your premise in my life
And now you blow in the bitter winds
Scathing and hungry, hunted for my sanity's keepsake

I do miss you

You know
Sometimes I miss you
I think about how exposed I got
I think about how really wild I got
I relish the thought of what we fantasised
And I wallow
Below
Somedays, when it's quiet
I go to that place
Where I've cast you far in the cage
Where your memory starves for us
And I let the minutes pass by softly
And I let myself miss you
To the marrow
I let myself be the girl that missed you
The one who was sad when it ended
The one who hated how new things became
The one who denied being heartbroken
The one who hid her tears and refused to cry
The one who slowly got over you
You know
I remember I got furious
At you for your callousness
I lament my deranged fear of heartbreak
I hate how fragile our love was
And how ridiculously careless we were
Had we been delicate with it
Well,
You know the rest

NINA MTANU

Your memory

When I think about us
Some days I remember and I'm furious
Some nights I recall and I'm so feverish
Sometimes I remember you and I get so sad
There were moments we were ravenous
There were times we let caution fly off
But then there are times I shared you
When I told others of you they saw
A version of you from the emotions
There were times they heard of you
And I had tears in my eyes
There were times they heard of you
And my voice had such joy
There were times they heard of you
And they seethed in solidarity
There were times they heard of you
And I was mixed up
But the way I remember you
Is always multifaceted
You visit me whenI need a hug
You visit me when I want calm
You visit me and I get so irritated
You visit and I find solace
And I can't say it out loud
They don't remember the times in between
They never were the ones dancing to the tune
They heard of you, but I was with you
Their accounts and mine differ

...

Just because
They have not seen your piled hurts
Drenched garments
Pained words on paper
Heard your wails at night
Seen you rammage through the many pockets for a drop of that love
Heard your heaves up the mount of pain
Doesn't mean
You haven't trekked through the dunes
Mirage of past lover's laugh haunting
Been sat alert thinking they might wave again
Been pelted with stinging denials and finality
Have sat in silence mourning your love
The sound of the farewell shot ringing
A smoking plume the memory it existsed
You laugh not like a wounded solider but a titan draped in daisy necklaces
Just because a love slumbers, loving morphs

NINA MTANU

Crossroads

At this chapters end
I'm realising that
Maybe,
I was able to finally close the door
Even,
When I wish I were somehow unique
Because,
You never called me by my name
And,
Anyone else after me
Could be called *'baby'* and it fit
Just fine

Part 3

LETTING GO

Save you

Sometimes in life
You're going to make hard choices
You will cry
You will want to quit
You will want the easy
But I won't lie
The best part
Lies on the other side
And only
You will save yourself
You will admit it to yourself
You will get up and move on yourself
Crying
Snotty nosed
In pain
So angry
Hating how unfair
Hating how foolish you feel
Hating how hard it feels like then
And it will be worth it

NINA MTANU

Enduring happiness

Because I've endured misery
You think I should be angry
Live burdened by bitterness
Wake and sleep loathing life?
What will that beget me?
Will tommorow come sooner?
Will I snatch happiness from it prior?
I mend what was torn in me
And live
Find the miniscule of happiness in today
And be happy to my core that day

Parts of me

The good
The works in progress
The bad habits constantly exhumed
The complete failures
The start overs
The new
These parts mold me daily

NINA MTANU

Phoneix

When your resolve
Shakes
And your mind
Wanders
Into the dark alleys
And hollowed terrain
When
Your will
Has wavered
Gasping
And grappling with defeat
Rebirth roams
The fevour to live
When gently rekindled
And nurtured
You will live and unsit
Those daring to trample it

...

When you regale them with the tales of us
Call me by my name
The wiry wilful one
With a mouth full of words
And eyes burning with determination
Don't hide my courage
In clipped pages of your illusions
Pour me a full cup
Of the adoration you hide
And sip at night in secret

Bounderies

The girl rolling in the grass
The woman howling at the moon
The girl dancing in the rain
The woman soaking in the quiet
The girl tired of facades
The woman living her truth
Gargle the discomforts
Pitch the refusals
And spit out the firey bounderies

Living

You've hidden
All the parts of you
All the cracks that shook
All the sparks that flew,
Churn the turbine
Come from exile
And live

To love

My love isn't always timid
It won't always shimmer
Some days it is the only thing
Some days it melds to others and they burn
Some days when I'm on, it rages, wild
It singes the very whispers of docile
It crawls through the halls of my fears
And when I have illuminated them
I bask in soft plush places of calm
I love kindly when I'm not rushed
I love gently even as I hurt at times
And when I have less in my cup
Some days I love tentatively
Some days I will offer broken love
Some days I love less and ask more
It is my dance in these fickle shoes
It is a dance that wears my soul out
It is a dance that has filled my soul at times

The free

Don't love me
When I look giddy
Talking about the things I love
Because it will reel you in
And when you grow tired of me
You'll think I'm too strange
And then you'll hate me
For being too free spirited
With a sharp tongue for truths

NINA MTANU

...

I remember you with sourness
Tangy and sharp
With mellow undertones,
Yet I wish
To remember you
Sweetly,
This is the brew of us

LOVE, LOSS & PEACE

Molt to grow

When you begin searching,
Within
You are going to dig, day after day
And you will find things
Discard things
And many of the things you will find,
Will only be pieces
So don't forget,
To stitch them with love
To glue them back witht the fond memories
And when you wash them
Scrub with care
Because even the most filthy parts
Helped conquer wars that led to where you stand a victor now

NINA MTANU

Eternal Love

In this life
We're told
'Everyone will find love'
So we spend all our life
Chasing love
But sometimes
The love of your life
Isn't living in that lifetime
Because this time
You're the one to love
You are supposed to be learning
To love you
Before they find you
Instead, we fall into pits, hollows
Drifting loves shifting facets
We question love
Discard love
We die before we really loved
Ourselves

Your art

This art of yours
I know it is beautiful
It speaks of things
But I don't understand it
But that doesn't mean
It is not profound
I am simply the wrong audience

NINA MTANU

Too much

I'm a conflict of emotions
Delicate sighs
And raging fears
Soft love
And blazing growls
Spilling over

Seasons in life

Some of them are intimate strangers
They know to navigate your dimly lit places
They heard you whisper to calm your demons
They have seen you shattered
They have witnessed you stiched together
Some of them are relative strangers
There was a time you needed them
There is a gaping hole in you they left
There is a role they should have played
There always will be a 'what if'
And you're whole
Even alone
Even mismatched
Even unfinished
Even building
You're whole

...

Worry not
About my curled fists
That clutch stardust
And tight lips
That vibrate with melodies
I'll sing at dawn
When my soul is at peace
Than pluck my heartstrings
For a crowd that boos my unique

Dignity

You are valuable
Every part of you is
You decide what price to sell it for

NINA MTANU

True to you

My life is my own
To love
To laugh
To cry
To lament
To fall
To rise
To nurutre
To examine
To grow
To rest
To push
But never to bargain for a drop of perfection

Your wings

In your laugh
In your eyes
In your words
In your small steps
In your big steps
All your little movements
All your boisterous takes
All your gentle loves
All your humbling stumbles
All your breathless fears
In your caged moments
In your unbelieveable times
In your weighed down gloom
In your soaring days
Glow from within

Rare

The less common i look
The better i feel
I'm a rare artifact

Self love

In the quiet nights
When you lay still and whispered
In the long days
When you yearned for it
In the splattering rain
When you tipped your head up
In the gathering
When you snuck a nibble of my charm
In the waking
When you longed for the solitude
In the bright sunlight
When you kept me close by your side
We laughed together
We lost ourselves in rhythm
We dreamed together
We sighed our wishes into the breeze
We cried together
You promised to always take me with you
Yours,
Self love

Kindness

Some of us
In this life
Have not known kindness
So they don't show it
But to live this life
You must teach yourself
To be kind

Also by Nina Mtanu

Love, Loss & Peace